TURMOIL IN AMERICA: THE 2020 ELECTION

Hal Marcovitz

San Diego, CA

About the Author

Hal Marcovitz is a former newspaper reporter and columnist who lives in Chalfont, Pennsylvania. He has written more than two hundred books for young readers.

Picture Credits:

Cover: Shutterstock.com
 4: Stratos Brilakis/Shutterstock.com (upper right)
   Tverdokhlib/Shutterstock.com (middle)
   Gemini Pro Studio/Shutterstock.com (bottom left)
 5: Stratos Brilakis/Shutterstock.com (upper right)
   Biksu Tong/Shutterstock.com (bottom right)
 8: Shealah Craighead/White House/ZUMA Press/
   Newscom
11: Juli Hansen/Shutterstock.com
13: Maverick Pictures/Shutterstock.com

17: Yasamin Jafari Tehrani/Shutterstock.com
21: lev radin/Shutterstock.com
25: lev radin/Shutterstock.com
30: NumenaStudios/Shutterstock.com
35: Rod Lamkey-CNP/Newscom
40: Sharkshock/Shutterstock.com
45: Associated Press
50: noamgalai/Shutterstock.com
52: Michael Nigro/ZUMA Press/Newscom
55: Consolidated News Photos/Newscom

LIBRARY OF CONGRESS CATALOGING-IN-PUBLICATION DATA

Names: Marcovitz, Hal, author.
Title: Turmoil in America : the 2020 election / by Hal Marcovitz.
Description: San Diego, CA : ReferencePoint Press, Inc., 2022. | Includes
   bibliographical references and index.
Identifiers: LCCN 2021014886 (print) | LCCN 2021014887 (ebook) | ISBN
   9781678202149 (library binding) | ISBN 9781678202156 (ebook)
Subjects: LCSH: Presidents--United States--Election--2020--Juvenile
   literature. | Elections--United States--History--Juvenile literature. |
   United States--Politics and government--2017---Juvenile literature.
Classification: LCC E912 .M373 2022 (print) | LCC E912 (ebook) | DDC
   324.973/0905--dc23
LC record available at https://lccn.loc.gov/2021014886
LC ebook record available at https://lccn.loc.gov/2021014887

CONTENTS

EVENTS SURROUNDING THE 2020 ELECTION

August 2020
On August 19 Senator Kamala Harris is nominated at the Democratic National Convention as Biden's running mate in the fall election.

July 2019
On July 25 US president Donald Trump pressures Ukrainian president Volodymyr Zelensky to announce an investigation into Hunter Biden, son of Joe Biden, who Trump anticipates will be his major opponent in the 2020 election.

February 2020
On February 5 the Republican-controlled US Senate votes to acquit Trump on the impeachment charges

On February 29 Joe Biden takes the lead for the Democratic nomination by winning the South Carolina primary.

2019   **2020**

December 2019
On December 18 the US House of Representatives votes to impeach Trump, finding that the president violated the law as well as the duties of his office in pressuring Zelensky.

On December 31 authorities in China acknowledge that they have treated numerous citizens of the city of Wuhan for severe flu-like symptoms; the disease, later named COVID-19, would soon emerge as a global pandemic.

May 2020
On May 15 the Trump administration announces plans for Operation Warp Speed, a $10 billion program to develop a vaccine for COVID-19.

On May 25 George Floyd, a Black man dies during his arrest in Minneapolis, Minnesota, when a White police officer presses his knee into Floyd's neck; the incident touches off national protests against racial injustice.

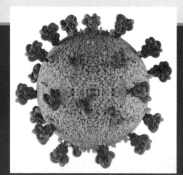

September 2020

On September 26 Trump hosts an event at the White House to announce his nomination of Amy Coney Barrett to the US Supreme Court; soon after the event, several attendees, including Trump, test positive for COVID-19.

On September 29 Trump and Biden participate in a nationally televised debate that is marked by incendiary rhetoric and personal attacks.

February 2021

On February 13, after a four-day trial, the Senate votes to acquit Trump.

2021

November 2020

On November 3 voters line up at the polls to cast their ballots for president and other elective offices; ultimately, 155 million Americans vote in the election.

On November 7 network TV analysts declare Biden the winner in the presidential race.

January 2021

On January 6, as Congress prepares to certify the Electoral College vote, Trump urges his supporters to march on the US Capitol, resulting in a siege on the seat of American government.

On January 13 the House impeaches Trump, this time for inciting the Capitol siege.

On January 20 Biden is inaugurated as president; Harris is inaugurated as vice president, becoming the first woman and woman of color to hold this post.

December 2020

On December 14 the Electoral College declares Biden the winner by a vote of 306–232.

Bitter Beginnings

No matter whether candidates are seeking seats on city councils, state legislatures, or in the US Congress, elections in America are rarely friendly affairs. They typically feature bitter fights between candidates whose views on how to solve society's problems differ greatly. Without question, the nation's election for president, which occurs every four years, usually features some of the harshest rhetoric and polarizing attacks that voters are likely to hear as they prepare to go to the polls.

As far as presidential elections go, perhaps no contest in recent memory conjured up the degree of incendiary campaigning more than the 2020 race. In October 2020, as election day neared, Michael Lewis, a professor of marketing at Emory University in Atlanta, Georgia, said, "Soon we will be inundated with speeches, policies, promises and advertisements for what might be the most hotly contested and divisive election on record."[1]

But the hostile nature of the 2020 race emerged long before the final few weeks of the presidential campaign. As far back as the summer of 2019, it became clear that the incumbent president, Republican Donald Trump, aimed to use all tactics at his disposal as he prepared for his reelection campaign the following year. Faced with poll numbers that projected him as the loser in the 2020 election to Democrat Joe Biden, the president resorted to a tactic that led to his impeachment—a measure pursued by Democrats in Congress to remove him from office.

The Call to Zelensky

In the summer of 2019, public opinion polls showed Trump suffering low approval ratings by voters. A June 2019 poll conducted by Quinnipiac University in Connecticut showed Trump trailing Biden, a former vice president, by a margin of 53–40 percent. Trump realized that if Biden went on to win the Democratic nomination, it would not be easy to make up the difference. And so Trump conceived a plan that he believed would cut into Biden's popularity among voters: he attempted to tie the Democrat to fraudulent activities committed by an executive of Burisma, a natural gas company in the eastern European nation of Ukraine. On July 25, 2019, Trump placed a call to Ukrainian president Volodymyr Zelensky in which he asked Zelensky to announce an investigation into Biden's son, Hunter, who sat on the Burisma board.

> "Soon we will be inundated with speeches, policies, promises and advertisements for what might be the most hotly contested and divisive election on record."[1]
>
> —Michael Lewis, professor of marketing at Emory University in Atlanta, Georgia

There had been no suggestion that Hunter Biden was connected to the crimes of the Burisma executive. But Trump believed that Zelensky's announcement of an investigation would make it easier to persuade voters that Hunter Biden was guilty and that Joe Biden had knowledge of his son's crimes. Therefore, the president could insist his opponent was a conspirator in the scandal. Moreover, another troubling fact soon surfaced: to pressure Zelensky into announcing the investigation into Hunter Biden, Trump withheld $400 million in military aid that Congress had appropriated to help Ukraine stave off attacks from Russia, its hostile neighbor. "The White House, the administration broke—I'm saying this—broke the law,"[2] Democratic House Speaker Nancy Pelosi said in January 2020. (Under law, the president is prohibited from withholding funds approved by Congress.)

By late 2019 the Democratic majority in the US House had initiated an investigation into Trump's call to Zelensky to determine

President Donald Trump meets with Ukraine president Volodymyr Zelensky (left) in 2019. Months earlier, Trump had pressured Zelensky to announce an investigation into Joe Biden's son for his possible connection to fraudulent activity at a Ukrainian company in order to undermine Biden's candidacy.

whether an impeachment vote should be taken. Impeachment is a process outlined in the US Constitution that gives Congress the power to determine whether a US president has violated the responsibilities of the office or has broken the law. Hearings were held in the House that included testimony from White House foreign policy experts who, as part of their duties, listened to the call between Trump and Zelensky. On December 18, 2019, the House voted to impeach Trump. No Republicans in the House voted for the impeachment.

Trump Survives Impeachment

The measure then moved to the US Senate, which held a trial on the charges. Several Democratic members of the House served as prosecutors, laying out the case before the Senate. To find the president guilty and remove him from office would take a two-thirds majority—sixty-seven votes—to convict the president. After listening to the evidence, however, the February 5, 2020, vote in the Republican-controlled Senate fell far short of sixty-seven votes to convict the president. All but one Republican member of the Senate, Mitt Romney of Utah, voted to acquit the president on the charge of abuse of power. On a second charge approved by the House—obstructing the House investigation—all Republican senators voted to acquit the president.

Trump remained in office and prepared now for the campaign ahead. But he was running now as a president who survived an impeachment—a factor that did not help his standing among many voters. He immediately went on the attack, attempting to paint the impeachment as a "witch hunt" orchestrated by his political opponents. He also mocked Biden, calling him "Sleepy Joe"[3]—clearly a reference to his opponent's age. (Shortly before the impeachment vote in the House, Biden had turned seventy-seven. Trump was not that much younger—at the time, he was seventy-three.)

Biden girded for a tough campaign ahead. As the months progressed, numerous attacks against the former vice president were lobbed by Trump. Several Democratic candidates also entered the presidential race, seeking their party's nomination. In the coming months the divisiveness that exists in American society would be exposed during the very bitter 2020 campaign for the presidency.

CHAPTER ONE

The Candidates

Although Donald Trump was acquitted in the Ukraine scandal by his Republican allies in the US Senate, some Republican leaders were incensed by his actions with regard to Ukraine. They also found fault with some of his other policies and decisions over the previous three years of his presidency. In fact, a group of Republican leaders formed an organization they named the Lincoln Project, through which they sought to undermine Trump's popularity among Republican voters. "Patriotism and the survival of our nation in the face of the crimes, corruption and corrosive nature of Donald Trump are a higher calling than mere politics," wrote the founders of the Lincoln Project in December 2019. "As Americans, we must stem the damage he and his followers are doing to the rule of law, the Constitution and the American character."[4] Among the founders of the Lincoln Project were John Kasich, a former governor of Ohio; Steve Schmidt, who managed the 2008 presidential campaign of Arizona senator John McCain; and George Conway, a prominent Washington, DC, attorney.

Trump faced opposition from other Republican leaders as well. In fact, by early February 2020, three opponents announced intentions to challenge Trump for the Republican nomination. They included William Weld, a former governor of Massachusetts; Mark Sanford, a former governor and member of Congress from South Carolina; and Roque De La Fuente, a wealthy entrepreneur from California. Trump promptly labeled his challengers the "Three Stooges"—a reference to the slapstick comedy trio that made numerous movies over a span of several decades. "They're a joke," Trump said of his opponents. "They're a laughingstock."[5]

Despite efforts by the Lincoln Project and his Republican opponents, Trump remained extremely popular among his core Republican voters. In early February voters started going to the polls to cast ballots in the presidential primaries and caucuses—the elections in each state that ultimately serve to select the nominees of the two major political parties. For example, in the New Hampshire primary, which was held on February 11, Trump scored 85 percent of the vote. His nearest challenger, Weld, received just 8 percent of the vote. Within the coming weeks, Weld and the other Republican challengers dropped out of the contest, clearing the way for Trump to easily win renomination as the Republican Party's candidate for president.

In December 2019, former governor of Ohio John Kasich (pictured) formed an organization called the Lincoln Project. The goal of the organization was to diminish Trump's popularity among Republican voters.

Clinton Urges Women to Run

While Trump cruised toward renomination on the Republican side, a much different contest was shaping up in the Democratic primaries and caucuses. By the time the voting commenced in early 2020, many Democratic candidates were well along in planning their campaigns. They had spent months raising money to finance their campaigns, purchasing commercial time on local and national TV broadcasts, and giving speeches laying out their positions on key issues.

Early on, the two main contenders were expected to be Joe Biden and Bernie Sanders, a US senator from Vermont. Both were veteran politicians, well known among voters and party leaders. Biden had served for thirty-six years in the US Senate representing his home state of Delaware before serving as vice president for eight years during the administration of President Barack Obama. Sanders was a former mayor of Burlington, Vermont's largest city. In 1990 he won election to the US House of Representatives, and in 2006 he won his first term in the US Senate. In 2016 Sanders campaigned for his party's nomination for president. Sanders waged a spirited battle, winning many primary contests, but he ultimately lost the nomination to Hillary Clinton, a former First Lady, US senator from New York, and secretary of state in the Obama administration.

Clinton was the first woman to be nominated by a major party for a presidential contest. And although she ultimately lost the 2016 race to Trump, shortly after the contest Clinton said she hoped her candidacy would help ignite the desire in other women to seek the nation's highest office. She said:

> Sometimes, the road to progress can feel like it's two steps forward, one step back, particularly when it comes

> "Sometimes, the road to progress can feel like it's two steps forward, one step back, particularly when it comes to advancing the rights, opportunities and full participation of women and girls."[6]
>
> —Hillary Clinton, 2016 Democratic nominee for president

to advancing the rights, opportunities and full partici- pation of women and girls. It can seem discouraging, whether you've been on that road for a long time or you're just starting out. But think how different the world would be today if the people who came before us had not just gotten discouraged, but because of that, had given up.[6]

In fact, several women did enter the 2020 race. Among them were four members of the US Senate: Elizabeth Warren of Massachusetts, Kamala Harris of California, Amy Klobuchar of Minnesota, and Kirsten Gillibrand of New York State. Also declaring her candidacy was Tulsi Gabbard, a member of the US House of Representatives from Hawaii.

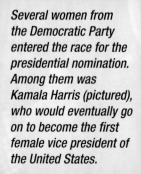

Several women from the Democratic Party entered the race for the presidential nomination. Among them was Kamala Harris (pictured), who would eventually go on to become the first female vice president of the United States.

A Diverse Field of Democratic Candidates

The list of Democratic candidates also reflected the various ethnicities, age groups, and sexual orientations that are found in the American electorate. There were two African American candidates: Senator Cory Booker of New Jersey and Deval Patrick, a former governor of Massachusetts. An Asian American businessman, Andrew Yang, entered the contest. A Latino, Julián Castro, entered the contest as well. Castro was a former mayor of San Antonio, Texas, who had served as secretary of transportation in the Obama administration.

A millennial, Pete Buttigieg, was among the early field of contenders. Millennials are members of a generation born from 1981 to 1996. (The name is applied to the generation because its members started reaching adulthood in the year 2000, the dawn of the new millennium.) Born in 1982, Buttigieg was serving as mayor of South Bend, Indiana, when he entered the presidential contest. In addition to being a member of a generation that is

Bernie Sanders: Democratic Socialist

Senator Bernie Sanders has twice made spirited campaigns for the Democratic nomination for president even though he is not a member of the Democratic Party. Rather, Sanders regards himself as a democratic socialist.

Socialism is a political philosophy that grew in appeal following the Russian Revolution of 1917, when the country's royal family was overthrown by activists who believed that all citizens should benefit equally from the nation's industrial output. The philosophy developed into communism, which endured for decades in what became the Soviet Union but eventually proved unworkable and collapsed in the breakup of the Soviet Union in 1991.

Democratic socialists have very much moderated the notion of modern socialism. Still, they contend that the economy should benefit all citizens, not just a wealthy few. Democratic socialists call for higher taxes on the wealthy and higher wages for working people. Sanders has also advocated for a health care system in which the government, rather than individual Americans, is responsible for most of the costs. Says Sanders, "We must recognize that in the 21st century, in the wealthiest country in the history of the world, economic rights are human rights. That is what I mean by democratic socialism."

Quoted in Tara Golshan, "Bernie Sanders's Definition of Democratic Socialism, Explained," Vox, June 12, 2019. www.vox.com.

underrepresented in most political offices, Buttigieg is gay and was very open about his sexual orientation.

There were many other candidates. By mid-2019, no fewer than twenty-nine prominent Democrats had announced they were at least exploring campaigning for the presidency. Among the candidates were two billionaires: Michael Bloomberg, a former mayor of New York City, and California environmental activist Tom Steyer. Both candidates announced they would devote portions of their significant wealth to financing their campaigns.

> "The Democratic field is so diverse compared to other years past because this year's field is reflective of its party's voters for the first time in a very long time."[7]
>
> —Harry Enten, political analyst

And so, as Democratic voters prepared to start casting their ballots in the presidential contest, they could choose among a very diverse field. Political analyst Harry Enten pointed out that the field of Democratic candidates reflected the ethnic and gender makeup of the voters of the Democratic Party. Polls around this time showed that about 25 percent of Democratic voters were straight White men, about 58 percent were women, about 10 percent were non-White, and nearly 10 percent were members of the LGBTQ community. "In other words," Enten said, "the Democratic field is so diverse compared to other years past because this year's field is reflective of its party's voters for the first time in a very long time."[7]

The Voting Begins

Still, despite the wide array of candidates entering the race in the weeks leading up to the early primaries and caucuses, Biden and Sanders were regarded as the front-runners. In January 2020 a national poll commissioned by the cable TV network CNN found Sanders leading the field with 27 percent and Biden close behind at 24 percent. Their nearest competitors were Warren at 14 percent and Buttigieg at 11 percent.

But then voters started casting ballots, and the results were hardly reflective of the early polls. The first test was on February 3, when the Iowa caucuses were staged. Iowa as well as other states stage caucuses rather than primaries—in caucuses, voters show up at school gymnasiums and similar venues where they publicly declare their support for candidates. In primaries, voters cast their votes as they do in general elections—in private voting booths. When the caucus votes were tallied in Iowa, Buttigieg emerged as a very narrow winner over Sanders. Warren finished third. Biden finished in fourth place. The next contest occurred two weeks later when New Hampshire voters cast ballots in their state's primary. This time, the winner was Sanders; Buttigieg finished a close second. Klobuchar and Warren followed. Biden finished fifth with just 8 percent of the vote. Clearly, the Biden campaign was in trouble.

Analysts blamed Biden's poor showing in Iowa and New Hampshire on mediocre campaigning. Biden failed to spend much time in either state in the weeks leading up to the elections. In the case of New Hampshire, aides to Biden acknowledged that the former vice president had long since conceded the primary to either Warren or Sanders, who represent neighboring states in the Senate. Said *Washington Post* political analyst Dan Balz, "If he truly wants to be president, he doesn't have to look far for answers as to what happened. His organization certainly failed him, but he contributed significantly to what happened [in Iowa and New Hampshire.]"[8]

Biden Takes the Lead

Starting with the next primary—South Carolina on February 29— the Biden campaign found new life. Biden finished first in South Carolina with nearly 49 percent of the vote. Sanders finished second with just 20 percent of the vote, well behind Biden. Steyer, who had poured $18 million of his own money into his campaign in South Carolina—most of it going into TV advertising—finished a distant third at just 11 percent.

US senator Bernie Sanders campaigns in Los Angeles for the 2020 presidential bid. A poll of voters in January 2020 showed Sanders as the frontrunner in the Democratic race.

Political analysts attributed Biden's victory to endorsements by several of South Carolina's African American political leaders. Most notable among this group was Jim Clyburn, a veteran member of the US House of Representatives and one of the state's most influential political leaders. In endorsing Biden, Clyburn cited the former vice president's long record of supporting civil rights legislation that had improved the lives of Black Americans. Black citizens make up a significant portion of South Carolina's Democratic voters, and their support is regarded as vital to a candidate's chances in the state. In endorsing Biden, Clyburn said, "I know his heart. I know who he is. I know what he is. I know where this country is: We are at an inflection point. I am fearful for the future of this country. I'm fearful for my daughters and their future, and their children and their children's future."[9]

> "I know [Joe Biden's] heart. I know who he is. I know what he is. I know where this country is."[9]
>
> —Jim Clyburn, member of the US House of Representatives from South Carolina

The Conways

Washington, DC, attorney George Conway is a founder of the Lincoln Project, which raised millions of dollars to work against the reelection of Donald Trump. He is married to Kellyanne Conway, who was Trump's campaign manager in 2016 and then served in the White House as senior counselor to the president.

The Conways married in 2001 and are the parents of four children. Their relationship was often tested during the Trump presidency as Kellyanne fulfilled her duties to advise the president while George worked to oust Trump from office. Reported the magazine *Vanity Fair*, "Kellyanne, who brought Donald Trump to victory in 2016 as his campaign manager, became, in her capacity as 'counselor,' his fiercest defender. . . . George became one of the president's most biting critics, with opinion pieces that shouted down Trump's disregard for the rule of law and tweets that pronounced him mentally unfit."

The couple's sixteen-year-old daughter, Claudia, often took her father's side, complaining about her mother's support for the president on her TikTok account, which has 1.7 million followers. Appearing on the TV show *American Idol* in February 2021, Claudia's complaints about her mother prompted *American Idol* judge and singer Katy Perry to ask, "Are you okay? Does she still hug you?"

Quoted in Evgenia Peretz, "State of the Union: Kellyanne Conway and George Conway," *Vanity Fair*, February 25, 2021. www.vanityfair.com.

Biden's strong showing in South Carolina helped the former vice president build momentum that ultimately resulted in the Democratic nomination. Voters cast ballots in primaries and caucuses for presidential candidates, but their real job in those contests is to pick delegates supporting those candidates who will vote at the national conventions staged by the two parties over the summer. Therefore, the primaries are really all about contests to pick delegates who are committed to the individual presidential candidates. And so, as the primaries moved into March, the Democratic field started shrinking as many candidates, unable to win many delegates in those races, started dropping out of the running.

On March 17 Biden emerged as his party's clear front-runner when he won primaries in three states—Florida, Illinois, and Arizona. Finally, in early June he had the nomination wrapped up, winning enough delegates to guarantee his nomination at that summer's national convention.

The race for the White House was now a contest between Trump and Biden. Earlier in the year, the campaign for the Republican nomination ended quickly as Trump's opponents soon dropped out after realizing the incumbent president enjoyed widespread support among Republican voters. On the Democratic side, the campaign endured for several months—but the candidates largely campaigned on their positions on the key issues that faced Americans. Personal attacks were largely not heard during the Democratic primaries and caucuses.

But that would soon change. Trump placed Biden squarely in his sights, leveling attacks at the Democrat that focused on his character and fitness for the presidency. Biden responded in kind. The 2020 campaign for the presidency was shaping up as a vicious battle that would redefine the culture of politics in America.

CHAPTER TWO

The Issues

As voters started participating in the early primaries and caucuses, they found the candidates taking vastly different positions on many of the issues that faced Americans in 2020. For example, on the issue of skyrocketing student debt—the tens of thousands of dollars many students must borrow to finance their college educations—Bernie Sanders declared that he would cancel all debt and that state universities should no longer charge tuition. Amy Klobuchar proposed severe restrictions on gun ownership in order to stem the rise of gun violence in America. Elizabeth Warren proposed a tax on wealthy Americans as a way of raising money to finance social services programs and pay for construction and repair of infrastructure. Joe Biden—who as vice president in the Obama administration helped craft the Affordable Care Act, which reduces the cost of health care for many Americans—proposed expanding the law in order to further reduce the costs of prescription drugs and other health care expenses for people.

Trump, meanwhile, rededicated himself to a plan to cease virtually all immigration from Mexico and other nations in Central and South America into the United States. He supported this policy by insisting that many immigrants take jobs from Americans or come here for the sole purpose of committing crimes. "When Mexico sends its people, they're not sending their best," Trump declared early in his political career. "They're bringing drugs. They're bringing crime. They're rapists. And some, I assume, are good people."[10]

National polling organizations confirmed that all those issues were certainly important to voters. Indeed, a poll taken on January 13, 2020, by the national polling firm Gallup reported that 81 percent of Americans believed affordable health care was the most important issue that should be addressed in the presidential race. Moreover, 74 percent of Americans said the issue of gun control was paramount in their minds.

But what no poll showed in January 2020 was the impact one issue would have on the race for president. It was an issue that would come to dominate people's lives even as the first votes were cast in the early primaries and caucuses. And that issue was a worldwide pandemic that would ultimately cost more than 560,000 American lives.

The Pandemic Hits the Nation

The pandemic emerged in late 2019 in the city of Wuhan, China, and quickly spread to other countries through travelers who, in the

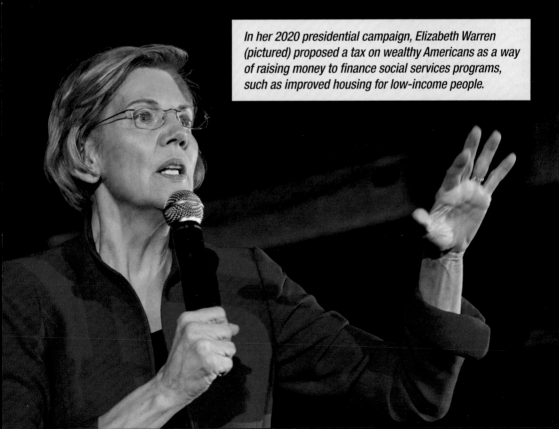

In her 2020 presidential campaign, Elizabeth Warren (pictured) proposed a tax on wealthy Americans as a way of raising money to finance social services programs, such as improved housing for low-income people.

early stages of the disease, were asymptomatic—meaning they did not display the symptoms and therefore did not know they were ill. Those symptoms included high fever, severe coughing, trouble breathing, fatigue, muscle aches, intense headaches, and the loss of the senses of taste and smell. The World Health Organization soon determined the disease was caused by a new type of coronavirus, spread through the germs expelled when people exhale, cough, or sneeze. The disease caused by the virus was named COVID-19, which stands for coronavirus disease of 2019.

Within weeks, tens of thousands of people around the world had become infected. National leaders in many countries ordered lockdowns, meaning people were not permitted to leave their homes except for the most vital of errands, such as shopping for food. As medical researchers frantically searched for a vaccine, the infection spread throughout America and other countries. And while most people afflicted with the virus recovered, many people did not. In America, by the time the primary election season had entered April 2020, some sixty-five thousand Americans had already died from COVID-19.

By then, Biden was the clear leader on the Democratic side. He characterized Trump's response to the pandemic as slipshod, contending that this response had resulted in many needless deaths. In fact, Trump had from the beginning attempted to downplay the seriousness of the pandemic, insisting that the disease would disappear on its own. He refused to heed the urgings of infectious disease experts, including some of his own advisers, to set a national virus response policy. Until vaccines were available, these experts warned, the best and only measures for protecting people was for all Americans to maintain social distancing guidelines—to stay at least 6 feet apart (1.8 m) from one another—and to wear face masks to protect themselves from germs floating in the air. Trump rarely wore a mask in public and mocked people who did.

And Trump insisted that an existing drug—hydroxychloroquine—was effective in minimizing the COVID-19 symptoms. The drug was developed to counter the effects of the tropical disease known

Trump Pledged to Bring Back Coal

While campaigning for president in 2016, Donald Trump pledged to revitalize the coal industry. "We're going to get those miners back to work," Trump said. "The miners of West Virginia and Pennsylvania . . . and all over are going to start to work again, believe me. They are going to be proud again to be miners."

But that did not happen. In January 2017, the month Trump took office, fifty-one thousand Americans were employed as coal miners. By November 2020 that number had dropped to thirty-nine thousand.

Over the past few decades, coal has lost appeal as an energy source because it is a major contributor to climate change. Phil Smith, communications director for the United Mine Workers of America—the labor union that represents many miners—says public utilities that generate electricity are hesitant to rely on coal out of fear that future laws will prohibit the fuel. He says, "When a utility is making a $3 billion dollar decision about how they're going to move forward and there's uncertainty that what's OK or approved now won't be in five to 10 years, under a different administration, they're going to take the path of least resistance."

Quoted in Céilí Doyle and Sheridan Hendrix, "Trump Promised to Bring Back Coal in Appalachia. Here's Why That Didn't Happen," *Columbus (OH) Dispatch*, October 21, 2020. www.dispatch.com.

as malaria. In fact, Trump acknowledged that he was taking the drug himself to prevent COVID-19 infection. "All I can tell you is so far I seem to be OK," Trump said. "I get a lot of tremendously positive news on the hydroxy. What do you have to lose?"[11] However, medical experts quickly declared that hydroxychloroquine has no properties that protect users against COVID-19.

Biden pointed out that during the pandemic, Trump's campaign insisted on staging large rallies in public arenas, such as sports venues. Thousands attended, and few Trump supporters wore masks. "He loves his rallies," Biden said. "But the next time he holds one, look closely. Trump keeps his distance. He's willing to let everyone in that crowd risk their life. But not him."[12] Unlike Trump, as COVID-19 spread across the country, Biden scaled back his in-person campaigning, instead remaining home in Delaware while making contact with voters largely through internet videoconferencing platforms.

However, the Trump administration did take some significant steps to defeat the pandemic, the most notable of which was a program it labeled Operation Warp Speed. This was a $10 billion program to assist pharmaceutical companies in the development, production, and distribution of vaccines to combat COVID-19. "Operation Warp Speed [will be] unlike anything our country has seen since the Manhattan Project,"[13] Trump declared. (The Manhattan Project was the military program established in 1942 to quickly develop an atomic bomb that was ultimately used to defeat Japan and end World War II three years later.) Trump announced the establishment of Operation Warp Speed on May 15, 2020. Within a few days, though, a much different issue surfaced, commanding the attention of the presidential candidates.

Marchers Demand Racial Justice

On May 25 the nation's focus shifted following the death of George Floyd, a Black man who was arrested for attempting to pay for a pack of cigarettes with a counterfeit twenty-dollar bill at a convenience store in Minneapolis, Minnesota. Floyd was wrestled to the street by four Minneapolis police officers and restrained for more than nine minutes while one of the officers, Derek Chauvin, pressed his knee into Floyd's neck. A witness recorded the arrest on cell phone video. The images clearly show Floyd in distress, pleading for his life, while Chauvin continued to apply the pressure on Floyd's neck. "Man, I can't breathe,"[14] Floyd said shortly before he died.

The video was uploaded to social media, where it was soon viewed by millions of people. The images prompted anger among Black citizens and others who have long believed that Black people are victims of systemic police abuse. Hours after the video aired, thousands of protesters took to the streets of Minneapolis and other cities to protest against racial injustice.

The Gallup poll that had been conducted in January ranked race relations in eleventh place among issues

"Man, I can't breathe."[14]

—George Floyd

Biden pointed out that during a pandemic, Trump's 2020 campaign insisted on staging large rallies in public arenas, such as this airport hanger in Pennsylvania in October. Thousands attended and not all Trump supporters wore masks.

Americans found most important in the presidential campaign. By early June it was clear that racial injustice had become a key issue in the presidential contest. Soon after the incident in Minneapolis, Chauvin and the other three officers were fired and eventually criminally charged in the death of Floyd. Biden called for the Federal Bureau of Investigation to investigate the case to ensure that the Floyd family received justice. He also called for a national campaign demanding that state and federal lawmakers improve existing laws to ensure that police do not abuse their authority. As Biden said,

> The pain is too immense for one community to bear alone. I believe it's the duty of every American to grapple with it and grapple with it now. With our complacency, our silence, we are complicit in perpetuating these cycles of violence. Nothing about this will be easy or comfortable, but if we simply allow this wound to scab over once more without treating the underlying injury, we'll never truly heal. The very soul of America is at stake.[15]

Trump focused more on the massive demonstrations that erupted following Floyd's death. In many cities, the demonstrations grew beyond peaceful protests as some participants vandalized and looted businesses that were along streets where the protests were staged. Over a period of several weeks, hundreds of demonstrators in several cities were arrested and charged with vandalism, theft, and arson. Trump vowed to send members of the military into American cities to take control and use firepower, if necessary, to quell the rioting. Four days after Floyd's death, Trump issued this statement: "These thugs are dishonoring the memory of George Floyd, and I won't let that happen. Just spoke to [Minnesota] Governor Tim Walz and told him that the military is with him all the way. Any difficulty and we will assume control but, when the looting starts, the shooting starts."[16]

> "Any difficulty and we will assume control but, when the looting starts, the shooting starts."[16]
>
> —Donald Trump

In making that comment, Trump sparked further anger in the Black community. The comment "when the looting starts, the shooting starts," was first uttered in 1967 by Miami, Florida, police Chief Walter Headley who was often accused of racism by the city's Black citizens. Headley made that comment as a warning to Blacks in his city during an era when demonstrations for racial equality were sweeping across American communities. Questioned after he made the comment, Trump said he did not know the history behind the remark.

Storms and Wildfires

By early summer the death of Floyd and the protests that followed served to make racial injustice a key issue in the presidential contest, but within weeks another issue began dominating people's lives. The summer of 2020 saw intense wildfires sweep across the western states, while people living in many eastern states found themselves victims of fierce hurricanes and other storms. Experts

During the campaign of 2020, Joe Biden pledged to end racial discrimination, but early on he found himself under fire for his opposition to the practice of busing. The term has been applied to the policies enacted by many cities to transport young Black students—on school buses—from low-achieving inner-city schools to more successful schools that are located in more upscale, and predominantly White, neighborhoods.

As a member of the US Senate in 1979, Biden supported legislation that prohibited the federal government from ordering communities to integrate schools by busing minority students into White neighborhoods. During the early debates for the Democratic nomination, presidential candidate Kamala Harris, an African American and US senator from California, lashed out at Biden. "You also worked with [segregationist senators] to oppose busing," Harris told Biden. "And there was a little girl in California who was part of the second class to integrate her public schools and she was bused to school every day. And that little girl was me." Biden responded that he did not oppose school integration but felt that it should be a matter for local communities to decide and that the federal government should not get involved in those decisions.

Quoted in P.R. Lockhart, "Joe Biden's Record on School Desegregation Busing, Explained," Vox, July 16, 2019. www.vox.com.

attributed the fires and storms to climate change—the heating of the earth's atmosphere caused by the burning of fossil fuels: oil, coal and natural gas. The burning of these fuels fills the atmosphere with so-called greenhouse gases, which serve to trap heat in the atmosphere much as a greenhouse traps sunlight to help plants grow. Climate change helps spark wildfires because higher temperatures tend to dry out trees and other vegetation, which makes them act like kindling if they are ignited by errant sparks. Climate change also fuels hurricanes because warmer oceans send a lot of moisture into the atmosphere, which helps make relatively mild rainstorms into fierce hurricanes.

In the January 2020 Gallup poll, just 55 percent of American voters regarded climate change as a key issue in the presidential contest. By late summer many voters were calling on the presidential candidates to take action to curb greenhouse gas emissions. Biden promised to rejoin the Paris Agreement, a treaty signed by 196 nations in 2016 to jointly address methods to reduce greenhouse gas emissions. Shortly after he took office in 2017, Trump ordered America to withdraw from the Paris Agreement. Trump complained then that the Paris Agreement was unfair to Americans in that it forced industries to cut back on their fuel consumption—and therefore their production—while industries in other countries could continue to burn fossil fuels. In fact, the agreement set targets but leaves it up to each country to decide how to reach those targets. "I was elected to represent the citizens of Pittsburgh, not Paris,"[17] Trump said when he ordered the United States to withdraw from the Paris Agreement.

Biden countered that the United States has to show leadership in reducing greenhouse gas emissions. He pledged to reduce these emissions to zero by 2050. He proposed reaching this goal by replacing cars and trucks that burn gasoline with electric vehicles and relying on renewable energy sources—such as solar and wind power—to replace coal- and gas-fired electric power plants. "We're going to combat climate change in a way we have not before,"[18] said Biden.

When it came to the issues debated in the 2020 campaign for president, the candidates took extremely different positions. On the issue of tackling COVID-19, Trump favored a hands-off policy, leaving most decisions to individual states and cities. Biden called for a national plan in line with the urgings of infectious disease and public health experts. On the issue of racial injustice, Biden called for a national policy to end systemic racism and police misconduct, while Trump declared he would send in the military, if necessary, to keep protesters off the streets. And as wildfires burned throughout the West and hurricanes raged in the East, the two men stood at opposite ends of the spectrum. Trump said reducing greenhouse gas emissions would force American industries to shut down, causing many workers to lose their jobs. In contrast, Biden pledged to eliminate greenhouse gas emissions within thirty years. As the contest headed into the final months before the election, voters knew very well where the candidates stood on the major issues facing the nation.

CHAPTER THREE

The Race Moves into the Fall

In every presidential election year, the major events of the summer include each party's nominating convention. The delegates elected in the previous months attend the conventions to officially vote on the nominations of the candidates. These conventions are typically held in major American cities and attended by thousands of people—the delegates, party leaders, other political insiders, and journalists. The conventions receive round-the-clock coverage in the media and culminate in nationally televised speeches by the party nominees on the final nights of the events.

But little of that happened in 2020. Because of the COVID-19 pandemic, both parties canceled their in-person conventions. The Republican and Democratic delegates voted over videoconferencing links to nominate Donald Trump and Joe Biden. Trump gave his acceptance speech from the lawn of the White House. About fifteen hundred supporters crowded onto the White House lawn to hear the speech, most not wearing masks or practicing social distancing. Biden accepted the Democratic nomination in a speech given from the stage at a sparsely attended event in his home city of Wilmington, Delaware. About thirty reporters were permitted to attend the speech in-person, although several hundred supporters gathered in a parking lot outside the Wilmington convention hall where Biden made the speech. During the acceptance speech, the attendees stayed in or near their vehicles and most wore masks during the event.

Kamala Harris (right) and Joe Biden (second from right) are pictured with their spouses on the night of Harris's nomination as the Democratic candidate for vice president. The nomination emerged as a major highlight of the Biden campaign.

Still, there was one moment at the virtual Democratic convention that emerged as a major highlight of the campaign. On the night of August 19, Senator Kamala Harris—who had been one of Biden's rivals for the nomination months earlier—was nominated as the Democratic Party's candidate for vice president. If elected, she would be the first woman and first woman of color to hold the office. (On the Republican side, Trump's running mate was the incumbent vice president, Mike Pence, a former Indiana governor who was elected with Trump in 2016.)

Biden had announced his selection of Harris as his running mate a week before the virtual convention convened. "I need someone working alongside me who is smart, tough, and ready to lead. Kamala is that person," Biden said. "I need someone who understands the pain that so many people in our nation are suffering. Whether they've lost their job, their business, a loved one to this virus."[19]

Harris's Aggressive Style

Biden's selection of Harris as his running mate in many ways reflected his response to issues that had been raised in the campaign. As a Black woman, Harris's presence on the ticket sent a message to the tens of thousands of police injustice protesters that Biden was serious about making racial equality a priority of his administration. Moreover, as a former prosecuting attorney, Harris was known for asking sharp questions during Senate hearings. During a debate between the Democratic candidates, she criticized Biden for his past opposition to the use of busing to achieve school integration.

Her aggressive style was seen as a boon to the ticket, inasmuch as Biden was known for a more laid-back style of campaigning. Harris's ability to snap back at Trump's attacks was welcomed by Biden supporters.

And, finally, during her career in the Senate, Harris made combating climate change a top priority. "Senator Harris campaigned fiercely for climate action in the past, and in the Senate, is a leader for environmental justice," said Joe Bonfiglio, president of the Washington, DC–based Environmental Defense Action Fund, a group that promotes clean energy. "This ticket shows just how committed Joe Biden is to making real and lasting climate progress and stands in stark contrast to Donald Trump and Mike Pence's efforts to implement a polluter-first agenda."[20]

> "Senator Harris campaigned fiercely for climate action in the past, and in the Senate, is a leader for environmental justice."[20]
>
> —Joe Bonfiglio, president of Environmental Defense Action Fund

Bitter Exchanges at the Debate

Following the virtual conventions, the campaigns moved into the fall, where they received nonstop coverage in the media. Biden and Harris made it clear they would attend few in-person campaign events due to COVID-19 restrictions. Whenever they did show up for in-person campaign stops, attendance at the events

31

was held to a minimum, and all members of the audiences were required to wear face masks and maintain social distancing.

This differed markedly from Trump's campaign. The president attended in-person rallies and other events where social distancing was largely ignored and mask wearing was not required. For example, on September 8 Trump spoke at a rally attended by several thousand supporters at Smith Reynolds Airport in Winston-Salem, North Carolina. It was an outdoor rally; nevertheless, months earlier North Carolina governor Roy Cooper had signed an order limiting outdoor gatherings to no more than fifty attendees—a regulation ignored by Trump's campaign organizers. "It's a great honor to be in North Carolina," Trump told the crowd. "We had great, great luck with people backing us in North Carolina. I'm thrilled to be in Winston-Salem with thousands of loyal hardworking patriots. You are great people."[21]

Biden and Trump both agreed to participate in presidential debates during the fall campaign. Typically, the debates are held in large auditoriums and attended by several hundred people. Moderators are usually network TV journalists. In 2020, though, attendance at the debates was severely restricted when Trump and Biden took the stage for the first debate on September 29 at Case Western Reserve University in Cleveland, Ohio. An estimated 73 million people watched the debate on TV.

What they saw quickly lapsed into a series of bitter exchanges between the two candidates. Trump was mostly focused on tying Biden to his son Hunter's business dealings in Ukraine—the issue that had resulted in his impeachment trial earlier in the year. "Your son goes in and he takes out billions of dollars," Trump charged. "He makes millions of dollars. What did he do with Burisma to deserve it?"[22] Biden snapped back, "My son did nothing wrong at Burisma."[23]

Trump Refuses to Condemn White Supremacists

The debate grew even more heated when Biden charged that Trump had done nothing to alleviate the tensions over racial in-

Following the 2016 presidential election, US intelligence officials concluded that Russian agents attempted to convince American voters to favor Trump, who Russian leaders believed would be a sympathetic ally to their regime. The agents posted phony stories on social media sites aimed at inciting anger against Democratic candidate Hillary Clinton.

In March 2021 US intelligence officials said the Russians made similar attempts in the 2020 election, but another country, Iran, also attempted to influence the election. In this case, the Iranians viewed Democrat Joe Biden as more sympathetic to their regime. Intelligence officials said they detected a campaign by Iran to send phony emails to voters in Florida and Alaska, purportedly written by members of the Proud Boys, a White supremacist group that threatened bodily harm to voters who cast their ballots for Biden. The intent of the emails was to gin up anger against Trump, who refused to denounce White supremacism. Said an email sent out to Alaska voters, "You are currently registered as a Democrat and we know this because we have gained access into the entire voting infrastructure. You will vote for Trump on Election Day or we will come after you."

Quoted in Sam Gringlas, "Voters in Florida and Alaska Receive Emails Warning 'Vote for Trump or Else!,'" National Public Radio, October 21, 2020. www.npr.org.

justice that erupted over the summer. Biden noted that Trump had, in fact, shown his support for White supremacist groups that believe in new measures to ensure segregation of the races. Among these groups are loose confederations of White supremacists that go by such names as the Three Percenters, Oath Keepers, Proud Boys, and Texas Freedom Force. In 2017 a rally of White supremacists in Charlottesville, Virginia, ended in violence. A young woman named Heather Heyer, who was participating in a counterprotest near the rally, was killed when White supremacist James Alex Fields Jr. purposely drove his car into the crowd. Fields later pleaded guilty to federal hate crimes and was sentenced to life imprisonment. Shortly after the rally, Trump refused to condemn the White supremacist movement. "You had some very bad people in that group," he said. "You also had some very fine people on both sides."[24] During the 2020 debate, Trump again refused to condemn the White supremacist movement, saying only that members of such groups should "stand back, stand by."[25] Many listeners interpreted that comment to mean that their presence could be needed in the future.

As the debate ground on, both men continued to trade heated rhetoric. Biden was clearly growing exasperated, though, because Trump kept interrupting his answers to the questions posed to him by the debate moderator, journalist Chris Wallace of Fox News. Finally, a frustrated Biden said, "Will you shut up, man? It's hard to get any word in with this clown."[26]

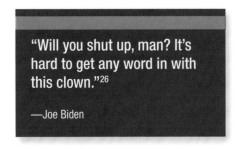

"Will you shut up, man? It's hard to get any word in with this clown."[26]

—Joe Biden

Following the debate, a poll commissioned by CNN found that 60 percent of viewers thought Biden performed better than Trump, providing voters with a clearer image of his vision on many major issues, including racial injustice, affordable health care, and a response to the COVID-19 pandemic. Just 28 percent believed Trump performed better than Biden. (The remainder of those polled had no opinion.) Moreover, in the first voter preference polls taken after the debate, the results showed that Trump continued to trail Biden—as he had since the primary and caucus season commenced some nine months earlier. For example, a poll commissioned by NBC News showed Biden leading Trump by eight points in the days following the debate.

Trump Contracts COVID-19

Three days before the debate with Biden, Trump staged an event on the White House lawn to announce his selection of federal judge Amy Coney Barrett for a seat on the US Supreme Court. The event was attended by hundreds of Washington officials and others. News coverage of the event showed that few people in attendance wore masks or maintained social distancing. Moreover, the reception that followed Trump's announcement soon moved inside the White House.

A week later eleven people who attended the ceremony tested positive for COVID-19. Medical experts labeled the event on the

White House lawn a "super-spreader," meaning the lack of masks and social distancing at the White House that day caused numerous people to contract the virus. "When you have large numbers of people spending time in close contact, unmasked, . . . it's a recipe for superspreading,"[27] says Joseph Allen, a public health researcher at Harvard University in Massachusetts.

> "When you have large numbers of people spending time in close contact, unmasked, and indoors, it's a recipe for superspreading."[27]
>
> —Joseph Allen, public health researcher at Harvard University

One of the people who tested positive for COVID-19 was Trump. Some medical experts speculated that Trump could have contracted the virus at the reception for Barrett. Others suggested that the president, who routinely eschewed wearing a mask or maintaining social distancing measures, could have been infected at any of several other events he attended in the days before he tested positive.

Trump staged an event for hundreds of people to announce his selection of federal Judge Amy Coney Barrett for a seat on the US Supreme Court. A week later, eleven people who attended the ceremony tested positive for COVID-19.

White House officials said the president was hospitalized after exhibiting minor symptoms of the disease. After three days Trump was released from the hospital, insisting he had returned to good health and was anxious to resume his campaign. He also maintained, as he had done since the earliest days of the pandemic, that the disease was not particularly serious. "Don't let it dominate you," Trump proclaimed after his release from the hospital. "Don't be afraid of it. You're going to beat it. We have the best medical equipment. We have the best medicines, all developed recently. . . . Don't let it dominate. Don't let it take over your lives. Don't let that happen."[28] The week that Trump made this comment, the Johns Hopkins Coronavirus Resource Center recorded more than 207,000 US deaths from COVID-19 and more than 1 million deaths worldwide.

Trump Claims Election Is Rigged

Following his return to active campaigning, Trump continued to trail in the polls. Another debate with Biden was held October 21. Following the debate, Trump again failed to improve his standing among voters. In the days leading up to the second debate, and during the final few weeks before the November 3 election, Trump floated a new theory before voters—that officials in numerous states were conspiring to rig the vote counts to ensure a Biden victory.

In America all elections are overseen by state governments—even elections in which candidates for president and other federal offices are on the ballot. Trump focused his criticism on state officials whose governments had eased restrictions on mail-in voting due to the pandemic. Typically, mail-in voting is permitted only for voters who have a valid reason for not going to the polls—such as making plans in advance to travel and therefore being away from home on Election Day. Many voters who cast so-called absentee ballots must apply for those ballots weeks before the election.

In many elections—particularly in presidential contests, which feature high turnouts of voters—polling places can be jammed with voters who wait in long lines to cast their ballots. Social dis-

Voters in some states found roadblocks as they tried to cast their ballots in 2020. These voters encountered fewer polling places, shorter hours, and rules requiring photo ID cards, such as driver's licenses. A report issued in September 2019 by the Washington, DC–based civil rights group Leadership Conference on Civil and Human Rights found that since 2013, states had closed some twelve hundred polling places. Most of those polling places were closed in African American communities in states that are controlled by Republican political leaders, the civil rights group said. "Moving or closing a polling place, particularly without notice or input from communities, disrupts our democracy," says Vanita Gupta, president of the organization. "It can mean the choice between picking up a child from school or voting."

An African American woman named Kathy waited in line for five hours to vote in the June 9 Georgia primary. She lives in the town of Union City, where the population is 88 percent African American. She said, "I'm now angry again, I'm frustrated again, and now I have an added emotion, which is anxiety."

Quoted in Andy Sullivan, "Southern US States Have Closed 1,200 Polling Places in Recent Years: Rights Group," Reuters, September 10, 2019. www.reuters.com.

Quoted in Stephen Fowler, "Why Do Nonwhite Georgia Voters Have to Wait in Line for Hours? Too Few Polling Places," National Public Radio, October 17, 2020. www.npr.org.

tancing can often not be achieved in those circumstances. And so, many states eased their rules on submitting absentee ballots, enabling virtually all voters to cast their ballots without physically showing up at their polling places.

Trump saw the submission of huge numbers of mail-in votes as a method to rig the outcome. He declared that there would be little oversight of the massive numbers of such ballots expected for the November election and that elections officials, meeting in secret, could falsify the returns. "Mail ballots are a very dangerous thing for this country, because they're cheaters," Trump declared. "Ripe for fraud and shouldn't be allowed."[29]

As Election Day approached, elections officials in numerous states defended the legitimacy of their processes

> "Mail ballots are a very dangerous thing for this country, because they're cheaters."[29]
>
> —Donald Trump

to collect and count the mail-in ballots. "Ensuring every South Dakota voter has access to exercise their right to vote is the goal of all election officials in our state,"[30] said Steve Barnett, secretary of state in South Dakota. In fact, Barnett said that months before the election, his office sent mail-in ballot applications to all South Dakota voters.

As voting began, Americans found themselves casting ballots in what was certainly one of the most bitter campaigns for the presidency ever waged in their country's history. And now, as the votes were being cast, a new shadow hung over the contest—the allegation by the nation's top elected leader that sinister forces were at work to deny him an electoral victory that he believed was rightfully his.

CHAPTER FOUR

The Votes Are Counted

As dawn broke on the morning of November 3, 2020, voters were already lining up at their polling places to cast ballots in the presidential election. Beth Michel waited in line for ninety minutes at her polling place in the Pittsburgh, Pennsylvania, suburb of Cranberry Township to cast her ballot for Trump. "He's an amazing man," she said. "The media image doesn't do him justice. He's my fan favorite."[31] Also waiting in line at the Cranberry Township polling place were Mary and Dennis Ritchey, who also voted for Trump. "We like Trump because promises made promises kept,"[32] said Mary Ritchey, who cited Trump's tough stance against illegal immigration and his support for the military as the reasons she voted for him.

In Atlanta, Georgia, Mark Robinson stood in line to vote for Joe Biden. Robinson said he was troubled by Trump's refusal to denounce White supremacist groups such as the Proud Boys and worried that if Trump ultimately lost the race, the outcome could spark violence. "I don't think I'm being pessimistic," he said. "I mean, the president said 'Stand back and stand by,' I'm presuming that's what [the Proud Boys] are doing."[33]

Although many voters waited until Election Day to cast their ballots, voting in the 2020 presidential election actually commenced weeks earlier. Due to the COVID-19 pandemic, many states initiated early voting options for their citizens,

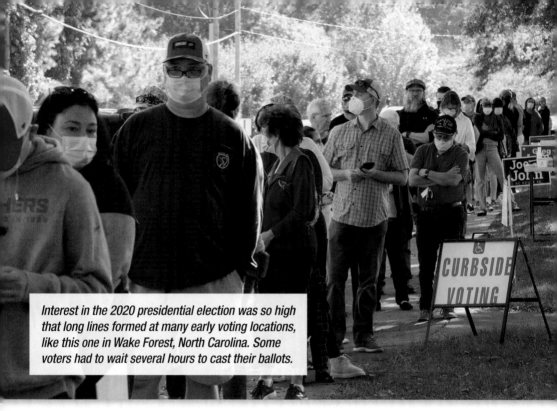

opening some polling places well before Election Day under the assumption that lines would be shorter and people could practice social distancing while waiting to vote. But interest in the 2020 election was so high that long lines formed at many early voting locations, making it difficult for those voters to maintain social distancing. Still, voters lined up—some waiting several hours to cast their ballots. In Atlanta, Georgia, Adrienne Crowley waited more than an hour to vote at her polling place on October 12—some three weeks before Election Day. "I would have waited all day if I had to,"[34] she said.

Trump Slows the Mail

In addition to permitting early in-person voting in response to the pandemic, many states encouraged people to cast mail-in ballots. And those ballots started flooding into state and county election offices weeks before Election Day. Trump remained convinced that mail-in ballots could be falsified, and he continued to rail against them for weeks prior to the election.

Moreover, Trump made the stunning admission prior to the election that he purposely delayed approval of the budget of the US Postal Service (USPS)—a federal agency—to slow the delivery of mail-in ballots to election offices so that the ballots would be delivered after Election Day. If the ballots arrived in the mail after Election Day, Trump believed—wrongly—that the ballots would not be counted. As early as August 2020, Trump acknowledged in a news interview that he purposely delayed approving the USPS's $26 billion budget in order to cause delays in mail deliveries. (The late approval of the budget caused the USPS to cut back on hours worked by letter carriers as well as delay the replacement of sorting machinery used to distribute the mail.) "They need that money in order to have the Post Office work so it can take all of these millions and millions of ballots. . . . That means they can't have universal mail-in voting. They just can't have it,"[35] Trump said.

Andrew Bates, a spokesperson for the Biden campaign, lashed out at Trump, charging that the president was not only interfering with legitimate ballots cast in an election but also slowing delivery of vital mail on which many Americans rely, such as medications and financial payments made by check. "The president of the United States is sabotaging a basic service that hundreds of millions of people rely upon, cutting a critical lifeline for rural economies and for delivery of medicines, because he wants to deprive Americans of their fundamental right to vote safely during the most catastrophic public health crisis in over 100 years,"[36] Bates said.

"The president of the United States is sabotaging a basic service that hundreds of millions of people rely upon."[36]

—Andrew Bates, Biden campaign spokesperson

Despite Trump's plan to slow the delivery of mail-in ballots, the USPS managed to deliver more than 65 million ballots cast by voters. In total, more than 155 million Americans voted in the 2020 election—making it the highest turnout for a presidential election in US history.

Despite his complaints that mailed-in ballots can be fraudulent, Donald Trump voted in the 2020 election by mail. A longtime New Yorker, in 2018 Trump officially changed his residence to Palm Beach, Florida. This is the location of Mar-a-Lago, the private country club he owns. To cast an in-person vote on Election Day, Trump would have had to travel to Florida and enter a polling place in Palm Beach. Instead, he remained at the White House in Washington, DC, on Election Day. In August—three months before the election—Trump cast an absentee ballot in the presidential race.

In fact, in the weeks leading up to the election, the media reported that at least twenty-four high-ranking members of the Trump administration also voted by mail, among them Vice President Mike Pence; the president's daughter Ivanka Trump and her husband, Jared Kushner, both of whom served as presidential advisers in the White House; and White House press secretary Kayleigh McEnany. Said Democratic vice presidential candidate Kamala Harris, "Donald Trump votes by mail but doesn't want you to. If it's good enough for him, it's good enough for us."

Quoted in Miles Parks, "Trump, While Attacking Mail Voting, Casts Mail Ballot Again," NPR, August 19, 2020. www.npr.org.

Biden Declared the Winner

Ordinarily, the results of the voting would be known shortly after the last polls close in the western states on the night of the election. Network and cable TV crews dispatch poll takers to key polling places, questioning voters as they leave the voting booths. These are known as exit polls—voters are asked their preferences in the election as they exit the polling places. The data gleaned from these exit polls is then examined by experts, who are usually able to project the eventual winners based in large part on the data gathered in the exit polls.

Moreover, tallies registered on voting machines are typically very quickly reported—particularly in recent years, since most counties have scrapped their mechanical voting devices and switched to computerized voting machines. With most computerized voting machines, when the last voter in line casts a ballot, the result is instantly reported to county election headquarters. Therefore, those network TV projections are also bolstered by the actual vote counts that are often reported soon after voting ends.

And while exit polls were taken in the 2020 race, and many of the machine counts were reported soon after the polls closed on election night, the experts held back on their projections because of the huge number of mail-in ballots that were cast in the presidential race. This meant that the TV broadcasters could not make their projections on election night. In fact, the results of the election were not known until November 7—four days after the polls closed. On that day—based on the reported machine counts and the tallies made of the mail-in votes—the TV analysts declared Biden the winner. "After four long tense days, we have reached a historic moment in this election," said CNN anchor Wolf Blitzer. "We can now project the winner of the presidential race."[37]

Ultimately, Biden received 81 million votes. Trump received 74 million votes. More significantly, Biden won the vote of the Electoral College—the process established in the US Constitution to decide the presidential election. The Electoral College is composed of representatives appointed by state governments. Each state is apportioned representatives according to its population. When the Electoral College meets following the election, its members cast ballots for the presidential

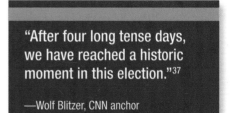

"After four long tense days, we have reached a historic moment in this election."[37]

—Wolf Blitzer, CNN anchor

candidates according to who won the popular vote in their state. (All but two states—Maine and Nebraska—award all their Electoral College votes to the winner of the popular vote, regardless of the margin. Maine and Nebraska apportion their Electoral College ballots according to each candidate's share of the votes.) In other words, if a candidate wins the popular vote in California, the state's fifty-five Electoral College votes are awarded to that candidate. California, as the nation's most populous state, holds the most Electoral College votes in the country. A much smaller state, such as Iowa, provides just six votes in the Electoral College. According to the popular vote recorded in each state, Biden won the Electoral College vote over Trump by a margin of 306 to 232. A minimum of 270 votes of the 538 Electoral College votes is necessary to win the presidency.

Trump Refuses to Concede

In the days following the election, Biden was declared the winner by TV analysts. Slowly, each state reported its official vote counts. And on December 14 the votes of the Electoral College were recorded in Biden's favor. But through it all, Trump refused to concede the election to Biden. In fact, for several days following the election, Trump refused to speak publicly about the race or answer questions from reporters on whether he had accepted Biden's victory.

Instead, former New York City mayor Rudy Giuliani—a close Trump ally—spoke for Trump, announcing that the president believed he had won the election and that many mail-in ballots were falsified to add to Biden's vote count. Although Giuliani offered no proof of this, he declared that the Trump campaign and its allies would file court challenges, seeking to overturn the results in several key states. Giuliani maintained that Trump led in the public opinion polls throughout the year—a position that was not supported by the numerous polls that gauged voter preferences in the contest. "You just don't lose leads like that without corruption,"[38] Giuliani insisted.

> "You just don't lose leads like that without corruption."[38]
>
> —Rudy Giuliani, attorney for Donald Trump

Over the next several weeks, the Trump campaign or local Republican leaders allied with Trump filed more than sixty lawsuits in county, state, and federal courts challenging the vote totals in Arizona, Georgia, Michigan, Nevada, and Pennsylvania—all states won by Biden. In every case, judges rejected the claims by the Trump campaign or the president's allies. In three cases, the decisions by the local judges were appealed to the US Supreme Court. In each case, the nation's highest court rejected the appeals.

Rudy Giuliani (pictured) announced that President Trump believed the election was fraudulent and declared that the Trump campaign would file court challenges seeking to overturn the results in several key states.

Most of the lawsuits challenged the way the mail-in ballots were counted. Among the complaints filed by the Trump campaign or local Republican leaders were decisions by state election officials to count ballots if they were received in the mail after Election Day. Those complaints were routinely dismissed by numerous judges. In Pennsylvania the Trump campaign challenged the counting of ballots in the city of Philadelphia, claiming the recording of the votes was conducted without Republican Party witnesses permitted to oversee the process. A judge rejected that complaint after the party acknowledged that Republican leaders had in fact been permitted to witness the counting process. In Wayne County, Michigan, a group of Republicans filed a lawsuit alleging widespread corruption in the vote-counting process but submitted no evidence backing up their claims. The Republican leaders asked the judge to order that the election be held again in

It is possible for a presidential candidate to win the popular vote but still lose the election. The US Constitution established the Electoral College to determine the winner of the presidency. Each state is allocated members of the Electoral College based on its population. Most states maintain "winner-take-all" policies, meaning that candidates who win elections by narrow margins still win all the state's electoral votes.

That policy has occasionally resulted in a candidate who lost the national popular vote to still win the presidency. A candidate who wins the popular vote in a large state, such as California, is awarded all of California's fifty-five Electoral College votes. Meanwhile, though, the opponent may have narrowly won the popular votes in numerous small states. Even though that candidate's margins of victories in those small states fall far short of his or her opponent's popular vote in California, those small state votes add up and can mean the difference in the Electoral College. It happened in 2016 when Hillary Clinton won the national popular vote over Donald Trump by 2.8 million votes, due largely to her commanding victories in large states such as California and New York. But in the Electoral College, Trump was declared the winner when he was awarded 306 votes to 232 for Clinton, thanks to the winner-take-all policies of smaller states he won by narrow margins.

Wayne County, but a judge rejected the request and dismissed the lawsuit. And in Maricopa County, Arizona, the Trump campaign alleged that scanning devices used to read the mail-in ballots did not work properly because many voters marked their ballots with Sharpie pens, which tend to make thick lines on paper. A judge dismissed the case, finding no evidence that the scanners misread the Sharpie-marked ballots.

Trump Pressures Georgia Officials

Following the election, no state received more pressure from the Trump campaign to reverse Biden's election win than Georgia. In Georgia the state government is led by Republican governor Brian Kemp—who supported Trump in the presidential campaign. In December and early January—as Georgia officials conducted the official count of ballots—Trump placed calls to Kemp as well as

Georgia secretary of state Brad Raffensperger, also a Republican, who oversees elections in Georgia, asking for help in finding more votes in the state. Biden beat Trump by a margin of 11,779 votes in Georgia, thereby winning the state's sixteen Electoral College votes. Trump told Raffensperger, "All I want to do is this. I just want to find 11,780 votes."[39]

But Kemp and Raffensperger refused the president's request. Raffensperger said he reminded the president that judges had dismissed five lawsuits challenging the outcome in Georgia. Raffensperger said he stood by the work performed by the elections staff members under his authority and that no evidence of fraud in the counting of the Georgia ballots had been found. Raffensperger said he told Trump, "We've had several lawsuits, and we've had to respond in court to the lawsuits and the contentions. We don't agree that you have won."[40]

Defeated at the polls, in the Electoral College, and in more than sixty lawsuits filed in five states, by early January Trump had seemingly exhausted all his paths to victory. None of the court challenges filed by his campaign or local Republican leaders proved to be valid. Meanwhile, at his headquarters in Wilmington, Delaware, Biden had been meeting with aides since shortly after the election to begin the process of establishing a new administration. Over the next few weeks, Biden planned to name new cabinet officials—the secretaries of state, defense, and the treasury, as well as other key posts in the new government. Meanwhile, at the US Capitol in Washington, DC, Republican and Democratic leaders in Congress prepared for the new administration as well, which was set to begin on January 20, 2021—the day Biden would be inaugurated as the forty-sixth president of the United States.

CHAPTER FIVE

The US Capitol Under Siege

Throughout November and December 2020 and into the early days of January 2021, as president-elect Joe Biden planned his new administration, Donald Trump steadfastly refused to concede the election. Moreover, Trump refused to make the resources of the federal government available to Biden to help the incoming president prepare to begin governing. The period between the election and the inauguration of a new president is unofficially known as the "transition." During this period, high-ranking officials in the current administration meet with the incoming president to provide briefings on the major issues the new president is sure to face following the inauguration. In the past, incumbent administrations have always worked closely with presidents-elect and their aides to ensure smooth transitions, which all participants have agreed is in the best interest of the country.

But for several weeks, Trump refused to make his aides and other top officials available for interviews with Biden. One of the top officials who traditionally meets with the incoming president is the secretary of state—the nation's chief diplomat. The secretary of state is expected to brief the incoming president on trouble spots around the world. This includes places where icy relations among neighboring nations may escalate into warfare or other places where anti-American feelings may endanger the lives of US citizens.

Following Trump's orders, Secretary of State Mike Pompeo refused to meet with Biden. Moreover, when questioned by reporters, Pompeo suggested that he agreed with Trump's belief that the election was stolen and that the court challenges then under

> **"There will be a smooth transition to a second Trump administration."[41]**
>
> —Mike Pompeo, US secretary of state

way would ultimately result in Trump remaining in office for a second term. "There will be a smooth transition to a second Trump administration,"[41] Pompeo told reporters a week after the election.

Challenge to the Electoral College

As Trump blocked the transition, and as the judges assigned to the election challenges continually dismissed the president's efforts to overturn the outcome, Trump's focus turned to a much different strategy. After the Electoral College certified Biden's win on December 14, under federal law one more step was necessary for the outcome of the election to be declared final. Members of the House and Senate were scheduled to meet in the US Capitol on January 6, 2021, in a joint session of Congress to conduct a formal count and acceptance of the Electoral College vote. Presiding over this special session of Congress would be the vice president.

In past years this session of Congress has been little more than a ceremonial event. At no time in the nation's history has Congress rejected the count of the Electoral College. In fact, in 2017 Biden, as vice president, presided over the joint session to accept Trump's victory in the Electoral College. But as the 2021 special session of Congress approached, Trump called for his allies in Congress to object to the vote of the Electoral College and ultimately to reject the outcome. Moreover, he called on Vice President Mike Pence to use his authority, while presiding over the joint session, to reject the Electoral College vote.

Fourteen current and incoming Republican members of the Senate said they would object to the Electoral College count. But even those senators said they expected their objections to fall far short of denying Biden the Electoral College victory. "We are not naive," the Republican senators said in a joint statement. "We fully expect most if not all Democrats, and perhaps more than a few Republicans, to vote otherwise." Yet again referring to unsubstantiated claims of election fraud, they added that "support of election integrity should not be a partisan issue."[42] When members of the House of Representatives had their say on the matter, 147 Republican House members voted against accepting the results of the Electoral College.

As for the vice president rejecting the Electoral College count, Pence said that while he would permit members of Congress to lodge objections to the vote, he would take no steps to personally overturn the count of the Electoral College. Constitutional scholars were quick to point out that Pence, even if he had wanted to, had no authority under law to do so. "One of the points of the Electoral Count Act is to constrain the vice president . . . and make it clear that he's a presider, not a decider,"[43] says Trevor Potter, the former

Following Trump's orders, Secretary of State Mike Pompeo initially refused to meet with Biden to ensure a smooth transition of power.

chair of the Federal Election Commission, the federal agency that serves as a watchdog over campaign fundraising and spending.

Speech on the Ellipse

Now that it was clear Trump lacked the votes in Congress to overturn the Electoral College result and that Pence would not block the final count

> "One of the points of the Electoral Count Act is to constrain the vice president . . . and make it clear that he's a presider, not a decider."[43]
>
> —Trevor Potter, former chair of the Federal Election Commission

of the official results, the outgoing president made a final plea to his most ardent supporters. He urged them to reject Biden's victory. Trump announced his plans to make a speech on January 6 at the Ellipse, a public park in Washington, DC, just a few blocks from the Capitol. The rally was organized by a group calling itself Stop the Steal. Composed of Trump supporters, the group's name was drawn from a slogan Trump had concocted over the previous weeks, suggesting that Biden's allies had rigged the outcome of the election and were stealing the presidency from him.

When the crowd of about a hundred thousand people started forming on the Ellipse that morning, it was clear that a number of the attendees were from the White supremacist movement. This was the same movement that had spawned the Proud Boys and similar groups that Trump had repeatedly refused to denounce during his presidency. Trump took the stage at about noon. During his speech to the crowd, he said he still had no intention of conceding the election to Biden. "You don't concede when there's theft involved," Trump declared. "Our country has had enough. We will not take it anymore."[44]

He then urged the crowd to march to the Capitol and demand that Congress overturn the results of the Electoral College. He told the crowd, "If you don't fight like hell you're not going to have a country anymore."[45]

> "You don't concede when there's theft involved."[44]
>
> —Donald Trump

51

Following those words, hundreds of his supporters did march to the Capitol, arriving at about one o'clock. At first, they surrounded the building and shouted demands for Congress to reject the Electoral College vote. But then things quickly got out of hand.

Ransacking the Capitol

The protesters were able to force their way inside the building, overpowering the few police officers who had been assigned to protect the building and its occupants that morning. Many protesters broke through doors; others smashed windows. Police officers were physically assaulted by the violent mob.

Within minutes hundreds of Trump supporters were roaming the halls of the Capitol building. They broke into offices, rifled through desk drawers, and generally ransacked the building. The office of US House Speaker Nancy Pelosi was targeted by the demonstrators. A longtime critic of Trump, Pelosi had backed the president's impeachment in 2020. Pelosi's office was ransacked, and a laptop computer was stolen from the office. One protester was photographed carrying off the lectern used by the Speaker to preside over meetings. And one protester was photographed sitting with his feet on the desk in Pelosi's office.

On January 6, 2021, hundreds of Trump supporters broke into the Capitol building. Within minutes, the protesters were roaming the halls and ransacking offices of top members of Congress. Many people had to barricade themselves in offices for their safety.

Casualties of the Capitol Siege

During the siege on the US Capitol, a police officer, Brian Sicknick, fell ill while defending the building against intruders. He later died. Authorities believe Sicknick was hit with a lethal dose of bear spray—a chemical repellant hikers use when they are confronted by bears in the wild.

In March 2021 two of the rioters were charged with assaulting Sicknick. They were identified as Julian Khater of State College, Pennsylvania, and George Tanios of Morgantown, West Virginia. Authorities said they examined videos and photographs from the siege and determined that Khater and Tanios fired the bear spray cannisters numerous times during the day. One video showed Sicknick and two other officers stricken by the repellant.

Four of the rioters also died in the melee. They included Benjamin Philips of Ringtown, Pennsylvania, who died of a stroke during the chaotic day; Rosanne Boyland of Kennesaw, Georgia, who died as she was crushed by rioters attempting to force their way into the Capitol; Kevin D. Greeson of Athens, Alabama, who suffered a fatal heart attack during the siege; and Ashli Babbitt of San Diego, California, who was shot by a police officer as she attempted to force her way in through a door of the Capitol.

Meanwhile, members of Congress who were meeting in the House Chamber were ordered by security officers to take cover. Many hid under desks. One member of the House, Alexandria Ocasio-Cortez of New York City, said later that she feared for her life during the siege. "I did not know if I was going to make it to the end of that day alive,"[46] she said.

Security officers in the Capitol were also concerned about the safety of Pence. He had defied the president's wishes to deny Biden the Electoral College count. In fact, during the riot Trump wrote on his Twitter account, "Mike Pence didn't have the courage to do what should have been done to protect our Country and our Constitution."[47] At about two o'clock, Pence and all members of Congress and their staffs were evacuated from the Capitol under heavy guard by security guards and Secret Service agents.

> "I did not know if I was going to make it to the end of that day alive."[46]
>
> —Alexandria Ocasio-Cortez, member of US House of Representatives from New York

In the days following the siege on the US Capitol images and video of one particular activist seemed to dominate the news. The activist, Jacob Chansley, was shown striding around the halls of the Capitol bare-chested with his face painted and wearing a fur headdress featuring prominent horns. Chansley, of Phoenix, Arizona, regards himself as a "QAnon shaman," meaning he believes he has inside access to the information promoted by the so-called QAnon movement—an underground sect that promotes bizarre conspiracies that warn of the takeover of the US government.

Soon after the siege Chansley was taken into custody, charged with civil disorder, obstruction of an official proceeding, violent entry, and disorderly conduct. Moreover, prosecutors alleged that he made threats against Vice President Mike Pence, who was criticized by President Trump for refusing to overturn the results of the Electoral College. By spring 2021 Chansley remained in jail awaiting trial. In turning down a request by Chansley's lawyer to release the defendant on bail, US District Judge Royce Lamberth said, "These are not the actions of a person who is shy about breaking the law."

Quoted in Jaclyn Diaz, "Jacob Chansley, Self-Styled 'QAnon Shaman,' to Stay in Jail Pending Trial," National Public Radio, March 9, 2021. npr.org.

Biden and Harris Inaugurated

Reinforcements were called in. Members of the Washington, DC, municipal police force as well as soldiers from the National Guard responded to the siege. By about four o'clock, the reinforcements had arrived at the Capitol. Many of the demonstrators still in the building at that time were arrested. Order was restored, and members of Congress returned to the Capitol later that night to complete the job of certifying the election. And in the early morning hours of January 7, the process was completed: Biden was certified as the winner of the 2020 presidential election.

Biden as well as Vice President Kamala Harris were inaugurated on January 20. Traditionally, presidential inaugurations are huge events that dominate Washington society for days. Tens of thousands of people ordinarily attend the inauguration, which is held on the steps of the Capitol. A parade follows, and later in the evening, grand balls are held, attended by the president and First Lady. But again, due to concerns about the pandemic, the crowd attending the ceremony on the Capitol steps was limited to just two hundred guests, all sitting 6 feet (1.8 m) apart and wearing masks. No parade or balls were held following the swearing-in ceremony.

Trump refused to attend the inauguration—becoming only the fourth president in US history to refuse to attend the inauguration of a successor. (The others were presidents John Adams, John Quincy Adams, and Andrew Johnson. As with Trump, all had been rejected by voters for second terms.)

The repercussions of the January 6 siege did not end with Biden's inauguration. In the days following the siege, law enforcement officers studied security camera footage of the riot as well as cell phone video many of the participants had posted on social media. Police started making arrests, and by March 2020 more than four hundred participants had been charged with crimes stemming from the Capitol siege.

Many members of Congress, convinced that Trump's incendiary words at the January 6 rally incited the crowd to lay siege to the Capitol, called for the president to be impeached a second time. In this case, a conviction following the impeachment trial

Joe Biden at his presidential inauguration on Capitol Hill on January 20, 2020. Trump refused to attend the inauguration, becoming only the fourth president in US history to refuse to attend the inauguration of a successor.

would not result in the removal of the president from office—the voters had already seen to that—but could bar Trump from seeking the presidency again.

The Second Impeachment

On January 13, 2020, one week before Biden's inauguration, the House voted to impeach Trump a second time. The vote was 232–197. Unlike the previous impeachment, this time ten Republican members of the House joined Democrats in voting to approve a single article of impeachment charging Trump with committing incitement of insurrection by urging the crowd to lay siege to the Capitol on January 6. Said the article of impeachment, "He threatened the integrity of the democratic system, interfered with the peaceful transition of power, and imperiled a coequal branch of government. He thereby betrayed his trust as president, to the manifest injury of the people of the United States."[48]

The Senate staged a trial on the impeachment charge commencing on February 9. The trial lasted four days. This time, Mitt Romney as well as six other Republican senators joined all Democrats in voting to convict the president. The final vote was 57–43 in favor of conviction. Again, though, the vote fell short of the two-thirds majority required for a conviction, resulting in an acquittal on the charge.

The vote to acquit the former president finally brought the tumultuous 2020 election for the presidency to an end. For all Americans, 2020 will remain a divisive year in politics—a year when a pandemic swept across the country, Black citizens and others marched for racial justice, and many Americans found their homes and even their lives in danger from the threat of climate change. But in the end, the American system of democracy prevailed. A fair election was held, and whether they cast their ballots in person or by mail, voters had their say in who should lead them for the next four years.

SOURCE NOTES

Introduction: Bitter Beginnings

1. Michael Lewis, "Playing Dirty in 2020—but Does Negative Advertising Actually Work in Elections?," Goizueta Business School, Emory University, October 27, 2020. https://goizueta.emory.edu.
2. Quoted in Susan Cornwell and Tim Ahmann, "Pelosi Says Trump Administration Broke Law in Withholding Ukraine Aid," Reuters, January 16, 2020. www.reuters.com.
3. Quoted in James Pindell, "Trump's 'Sleepy Joe' Nickname for Biden Isn't Working. Even Trump Knows It," *Boston Globe*, July 20, 2020. www.bostonglobe.com.

Chapter One: The Candidates

4. Quoted in William Cummings, "George Conway, Other Conservatives, Launch Lincoln Project Super PAC to 'Defeat Trump,'" *USA Today*, December 17, 2019. www.usatoday.com.
5. Quoted in Steve Holland, "Trump Labels Republican Presidential Challengers 'the Three Stooges,'" Reuters, September 9, 2019. www.reuters.com.
6. Quoted in Madeline Conway, "Hillary Clinton: I Hope a 'Wave of Young Women' Run for Office," Politico, March 7, 2017. www.politico.com.
7. Harry Enten, "The 2020 Democratic Field Is the Most Diverse Ever," CNN, January 27, 2019. www.cnn.com.
8. Dan Balz, "Joe Biden's Campaign Has a Problem, and It Begins with the Candidate," *Washington Post*, February 6, 2020. www.washingtonpost.com.
9. Quoted in Eric Bradner and Paul LeBlanc, "South Carolina Rep. Jim Clyburn Endorses Joe Biden Ahead of Primary," CNN, February 26, 2020. www.cnn.com.

Chapter Two: The Issues

10. Quoted in Gregory Korte and Alan Gomez, "Trump Ramps Up Rhetoric on Undocumented Immigrants: 'These Aren't People. These are Animals,'" *USA Today*, May 16, 2018. www.usatoday.com.
11. Quoted in Annie Karni and Katie Thomas, "Trump Says He's Taking Hydroxychloroquine, Prompting Warning from Health Experts," *New York Times*, May 18, 2020. www.nytimes.com.
12. Quoted in Trevor Hunnicutt and Jeff Mason, "Biden Bashes Trump's Leadership on Pandemic, Trump Attacks Biden on Trade," Reuters, September 21, 2020. www.reuters.com.

13. Quoted in Lauran Neergaard and Zeke Miller, "US Begins 'Warp Speed' Vaccine Push as Studies Ramp Up," AP News, May 15, 2020. https://apnews.com.
14. Quoted in Omar Jimenez, "New Police Body Camera Footage Reveals George Floyd's Last Words Were 'I Can't Breathe,'" CNN, July 15, 2020. www.cnn.com.
15. Quoted in Alana Wise, "Biden Calls George Floyd Killing 'an Act of Brutality,'" NPR, May 29, 2020. www.npr.org.
16. Quoted in Wise, "Biden Calls George Floyd Killing 'an Act of Brutality.'"
17. Quoted in Emily Holden, "What the US Exiting the Paris Climate Agreement Means," *The Guardian* (Manchester, UK), July 27, 2020. www.theguardian.com.
18. Quoted in Coral Davenport and Lisa Friedman, "Biden Cancels Keystone XL Pipeline and Rejoins Paris Climate Agreement," *New York Times*, January 20, 2021. www.nytimes.com.

Chapter Three: The Race Moves into the Fall

19. Quoted in Adam Edelman et al., "Kamala Harris Named by Joe Biden as His VP Pick," NBC News, August 11, 2020. www.nbcnews.com.
20. Quoted in Bart Jansen, "From Rival to Running Mate: What 'Fearless Fighter' Kamala Harris Brings to Joe Biden's Ticket," *USA Today*, August 11, 2020. www.usatoday.com.
21. Quoted in Carrie Hodgin, "President Trump Holds Campaign Rally in North Carolina," WWL TV, September 9, 2020. www.wwltv.com.
22. Quoted in Lisa Hagen, "Trump Forces Biden to Defend Hunter Biden's Record," *U.S. News & World Report*, September 29, 2020. www.usnews.com.
23. Quoted in Dave Boyer, "Biden Says Son Hunter 'Did Nothing Wrong' in Ukraine," *Washington Times*, September 29, 2020. www.washingtontimes.com.
24. Quoted in Meghan Keneally, "What to Know About the Violent Charlottesville Protests and Anniversary Rallies," ABC News, August 8, 2018. https://abcnews.go.com.
25. Quoted in Jonathan Lemire et al., "Chaotic First Debate: Taunts Overpower Trump, Biden Visions," AP News, September 30, 2020. https://apnews.com.
26. Quoted in Grace Segers et al., "First Debate Descends into Chaos as Trump and Biden Exchange Attacks," CBS News, September 30, 2020. www.cbsnews.com.
27. Quoted in Brian Resnick, "Was the White House Reception for Amy Coney Barrett a Superspreading Event?," Vox, October 3, 2020. www.vox.com.
28. Quoted in Morgan Chalfant, "Trump Tells Americans Following His Hospital Release: Don't Let Coronavirus 'Dominate You,'" *The Hill* (Washington, DC), October 5, 2020. https://thehill.com.
29. Quoted in Brandy Zadrozny, "For Trump's 'Rigged' Election Claims, an Online Megaphone Awaits," NBC News, October 15, 2020. www.nbcnews.com.

30. Quoted in Tyler Olson, "South Dakota Mail-In Voting: What to Know," Fox News, October 7, 2020. www.foxnews.com.

Chapter Four: The Votes Are Counted

31. Quoted in Don Hopey, "Live Regional Updates: 'We May Not Know the Results Today,' Gov. Wolf Says," *Pittsburgh (PA) Post-Gazette*, November 3, 2020. www.post-gazette.com.
32. Quoted in Hopey, "Live Regional Updates."
33. Quoted in Sarah Lyall, "How Long Is This Going to Take? Americans Settle In to Wait," *New York Times*, November 3, 2020. www.nytimes.com.
34. Quoted in Sam Levine, "More than 10-Hour Wait and Long Lines as Early Voting Starts in Georgia," *The Guardian* (Manchester, UK), October 12, 2020. www.theguardian.com.
35. Quoted in Sam Levine, "Trump Admits He Is Undermining USPS to Make It Harder to Vote by Mail," *The Guardian* (Manchester, UK), August 13, 2020. www.theguardian.com.
36. Quoted in Levine, "Trump Admits He Is Undermining USPS to Make It Harder to Vote by Mail."
37. Quoted in Ted Johnson, "The Moment When Networks Called the Presidential Race for Joe Biden," MSN, November 7, 2020. www.msn.com.
38. Quoted in Audrey McNamara, "Rudy Giuliani Says Trump Will Not Concede Election," CBS News, November 8, 2020. www.cbsnews.com.
39. Quoted in Ben Nadler, "Trump Pressured Georgia to 'Find the Fraud' in Earlier Call," AP News, January 9, 2021. https://apnews.com.
40. Quoted in Nadler, "Trump Pressured Georgia to 'Find the Fraud' in Earlier Call."

Chapter Five: The US Capitol Under Siege

41. Quoted in Bill Chappell, "Pompeo Promises 'a Smooth Transition to a Second Trump Administration,'" NPR, November 10, 2020. www.npr.org.
42. Quoted in ABC 7 News, "Ted Cruz Among Senators to Object to Electoral College Certification of Joe Biden Presidency," January 2, 2021. https://abc7news.com.
43. Quoted in Jane C. Timm, "Fact Check: No, Pence Can't Overturn the Election Results," NBC News, January 5, 2021. www.nbcnews.com.
44. Quoted in Sam Cabral, "Capitol Riots: Did Trump's Words at Rally Incite Violence?," BBC, February 14, 2020. www.bbc.com.
45. Quoted in Cabral, "Capitol Riots."
46. Quoted in Yuliya Talmazan, "AOC Says She Feared for Her Life During Capitol Riot: 'I Thought I Was Going to Die,'" NBC News, January 13, 2020. www.nbcnews.com.
47. Quoted in Marc Ambinder, "Trump's Actions During the Capitol Riot Put Pence in Danger—and National Security at Risk," MSNBC, February 13, 2020. www.msnbc.com.
48. Quoted in Lauren Egan and Rebecca Shabad, "House Impeaches Trump for Second Time; Senate Must Now Weigh Conviction," NBC News, January 13, 2021. www.nbcnews.com.

FOR FURTHER RESEARCH

Books

Jonathan Allen and Amie Parnes, *Lucky: How Joe Biden Barely Won the Presidency*. New York: Crown, 2021.

Victor Davis Hanson, *The Case for Trump*. New York: Basic Books, 2020.

Ezra Klein, *Why We're Polarized*. New York: Avid Reader, 2020.

Dan Morain, *Kamala's Way: An American Life*. New York: Simon & Schuster, 2021.

Evan Osnos, *Joe Biden: The Life, the Run, and What Matters Now*. New York: Scribner, 2020.

Internet Sources

Sam Cabral, "Capitol Riots: Did Trump's Words at Rally Incite Violence?," BBC, February 14, 2020. www.bbc.com.

Madeline Conway, "Hillary Clinton: I Hope a 'Wave of Young Women' Run for Office," Politico, March 7, 2017. www.politico.com.

Emily Holden, "What the US Exiting the Paris Climate Agreement Means," *The Guardian* (Manchester, UK), July 27, 2020. www.theguardian.com.

Bart Jansen, "From Rival to Running Mate: What 'Fearless Fighter' Kamala Harris Brings to Joe Biden's Ticket," *USA Today*, August 11, 2020. www.usatoday.com.

Brian Resnick, "Was the White House Reception for Amy Coney Barrett a Superspreading Event?," Vox, October 3, 2020. www.vox.com.

Websites

Democratic National Committee
https://democrats.org

Maintained by the Democratic National Committee, this website provides visitors with the party's positions on numerous issues. By accessing the link for "Where We Stand," visitors can read essays about how party leaders hope to provide affordable health care, address climate change, eliminate systemic racism from American police departments, and enable immigrants to legally travel to America.

Donald J. Trump
www.donaldjtrump.com

After leaving the White House, former president Donald Trump established this website to keep his supporters informed of his plans. By accessing the tab for "News" on the website, visitors can read Trump's commentaries on recent news events as well as his endorsements for candidates in upcoming elections.

Gallup
https://news.gallup.com

The website of the national polling firm Gallup provides results of public opinion polls taken on numerous issues, including voter preferences in upcoming elections. By accessing the tab for "Presidential Job Approval," visitors can see how Americans view the policies of the incumbent president. The presidential approval poll is updated every two weeks.

Impeachment Related Publications
www.govinfo.gov/collection/impeachment-related-publications

Govinfo is a service of the US Government Publishing Office. It provides free public access to official publications from all three branches of the federal government. This website has bills, rules, precedents, and other documents related to impeachment inquiries and proceedings. This includes the two Trump impeachments and select past impeachments.

Republican National Committee
www.gop.com

The Republican National Committee maintains this website to provide the party's positions on many national issues, including immigration and the federal government's response to the COVID-19 pandemic. By accessing the "Research" link on the website, visitors can find numerous essays on race relations written by Black commentators who have joined the Republican Party.

White House
www.whitehouse.gov

The official website of the White House provides profiles of major figures in the administration of President Joe Biden, including Biden, First Lady Jill Biden, Vice President Kamala Harris, and Second Gentleman Douglas Emhoff. By accessing the tab for "Priorities," visitors can find the administration's position on climate change, racial justice, COVID-19 vaccinations, and other issues.

INDEX